Nehemiah

Olwyn Harris

Reflections on a man who persisted
with rebuilding a vision against impossible odds

Suitable for Individual and Group Discussion

Copyright © Olwyn Harris 2025

ISBN   Softcover   978-1-923021-48-8
        eBook   978-1-923021-49-5

All rights reserved. No part of this book may be reproduced or transmitted in any form or by any means, electronic, or mechanical, including photocopying, recording or by any information storage and retrieval system without the permission in writing by the copyright owner.

Unless otherwise stated Scriptures quoted here are from the King James Version (Authorised version). First published in 1611. Quoted from the KJV Classic Reference Bible, copyright 1983 by the Zondervan Corporation.

Published by: Reading Stones Publishing
Helen Brown & Wendy Wood
Woodwendy1982.wixsite.com/readingstones
Cover Design: Olwyn Harris

For more copies contact the publisher at:
Glenburnie
212 Glenburnie Road
ROB ROY NSW 2360
Mobile: 0422 577 663
Email: Readingstonespublishing@gmail.com

Acknowledgements:

My heartfelt appreciation to Pastor Dawn Peel, emeritus, who has held a role supporting the credentialling of pastors within the Australian Christian Churches Movement. Thank you for your willingness to cast your theological eye over these chapters.

Table of Contents

Nehemiah ....

- Table of Contents 3
- Introduction 5
- The Vision was Caught 7
- The Mission was Accepted 17
- Gaps and Needs were assessed 23
- Opposition was overcome 28
- The Wall Structure was Rebuilt 40
- Processes were Reinstated 52
- Culture Re-established. 60
- Spiritual strength was developed 67
- Town was reoccupied 79
- Ceremony and Celebration 84
- Ongoing Process of Checking the Vision 89
- Appendix A 105
- Endnotes 107

Introduction

Taking time to reflect on the stories in the Bible, is something that we are encouraged to do in our walk with Jesus. I don't know anyone who would suggest this is not an important aspect of being a disciple of Jesus. Yet I have noticed, over and over, there is a widespread illiteracy regarding the stories in the Bible which I grew up with. I've also noticed that this unfamiliarity is not restricted to new Christians. I suspect we are more comfortable with the popular narratives on our TV streaming service, than the ones in our Bible.

The Holy Spirit, in his wisdom, has chosen the platform of storytelling as one way to communicate our spiritual relationship him, packed with wisdom, truth, morality, and values. It is not the only way God speaks to us, yet so much practical wisdom can be distilled from these narratives. Our challenge is how to access these stories in a way that allows them to be understandable in a world that is so far removed from the times when these accounts occurred. This series on *Reflections in the Bible* is not intended to be an exercise in theological exegesis, rather to create an opportunity to explore some of these stories. It is an invitation to go on a journey of reflection around what is described. What can we distil from these life-stories that makes sense for us today? Some of these narratives may be familiar. Some of them may be forgotten. Some of them are hard to understand. This is an opportunity to take time to slow down, invite the Holy Spirit to whisper his insight as we explore some of the stories he has preserved for us.

This book is intended to be a reflective space to use alongside your Bible. Sometimes, even the act of opening the pages of our Bible can be a challenge. So open up! Don't skip over the suggested passages marked as "Bible Readings". The scriptures tagged as "Bible Reference" are intended to bookmark passages, if you want to check them. Take hold of the opportunity to read or revisit God's Word. You are invited to use these pages as a place to scribble in margins; explore your own questions; and use reflective prompts to go a little deeper. My prayer is that it will be a springboard to explore the incredible love story of God, his great good news of redemption and His grace will draw you closer to who He is as our Good Father. I trust it moves each of us to appreciate more about our relationship with God, ourselves and life in community.

I.

The Vision was Caught

The story of Nehemiah is a story of rebuilding. There are many situations where we can see where rebuilding is necessary. It might be a neglected garden, or a rundown business, or a community after a natural disaster. It might be rebuilding mental health resilience or health and fitness. It might be a marriage falling apart or a family relationship in tatters, or even a fractured faith community.

What do I need to rebuild to align my life with what God desires for me?

I remember a conversation with someone who was in a rebuilding appointment with an organisation, and she very emphatically said that she would rather give birth in a labour-ward than try and do a resurrection. Rebuilding was not for her. Rebuilding is hard and challenging.

I remember going on a family holiday before we moved to take up a church appointment to rebuild. I was walking along a long, deserted beach, and I remember the tumble of the surf reflecting my own turmoil as I cried out to God. The task seemed so overwhelming. I didn't have a plan.

I knew I had to start, and I knew part of my call was to be a "Nehemiah". But I didn't know the story of Nehemiah very well. I knew he rebuilt the walls of Jerusalem in a remarkable 52 days and I had heard messages that leant into that idea to inspire great acts of impossibility. But it sounded so incomplete and not at all like me. That walk on the beach encouraged me to dive into the pages of Nehemiah and to explore how he had approached his mission of rebuilding. And what I discovered was so much more than 52 days!

The idea of rebuilding is not a unique situation for Nehemiah. This is something that has been part of the story of God's people in the Kingdom of God through many of the stories that God has given to us in his word.

Adam and Eve had to go out rebuild what was lost in the garden.
Bible Reference:
Genesis 3:23

Noah rebuilt what was devastated from the flood.
Bible Reference:
Genesis 8:15-17

Jacob rebuilt his flocks after fleeing for his life.
Bible Reference:
Genesis 30:25-43

Joseph rebuilt his life after being sold into slavery.
Bible Reference:
Genesis 41:45-46

Sometimes what was built was patterned after the template of what was lost, sometimes it looked quite different.

What I uncovered as I opened the pages of Nehemiah was more than repairing a demolished wall with bricks and mortar in 52 days. There is no doubt what was accomplished in that timeframe is a remarkable achievement, amazing! But this is not all it was. What I found was a framework of rebuilding an incredible vision imparted by God. In reality Nehemiah was commissioned as the governor of Jerusalem for twelve years. Rebuilding was not a 52-day super-exercise, but a long commitment of standing firm in his God-given vision and call. Rebuilding is multi-dimensional: It was a pledge to have strong foundations, strong structures: physically, culturally, spiritually. It is not just about a wall. The stages in rebuilding that I identified from the account of Nehemiah are outlined in Appendix A. Using this template from the account of Nehemiah, we will explore what we can learn about rebuilding.

Some Background...

I would like to start by looking at where this account of Nehemiah fits into the story of the Israelites; the big brush strokes. What we notice is that it quickly becomes quite complicated, so I made an attempt, like a wall, build up the picture of context to have some idea of how it all fits together.

Exile in Babylon	1st Return to Jerusalem	Genocide Attempt	2nd Return to Jerusalem	3rd Return to Jerusalem
	540 BC			444 BC

We start with the main events that happened so we can appreciate why Jerusalem needed to be rebuilt in the first place. Nehemiah's story does not happen in isolation. There were other people, previous initiatives and previous strategies. This was the third attempt to rebuild and reoccupy Jerusalem from when it was decimated from the Babylonian conquest under Nebuchadnezzar. In the interim there was an attempt to wipe out all Jews from the Empire completely which happened under the hand of Hamann, an account that is found in the story of Esther.

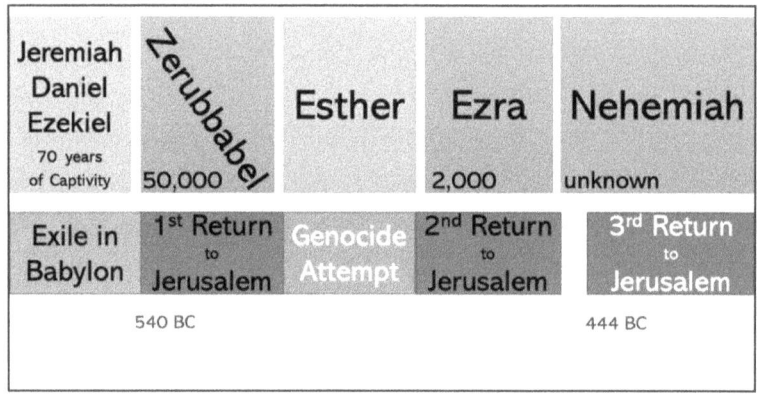

These are the primary Biblical characters we see during this period – all who are living during this period as the world power moves from the Babylonian Empire to the Persian Empire. Each one has a heart to honour God where He had positioned them. Zerubbabel became the first Jewish Governor of Jerusalem after the exile, and he led the first return from exile of about 50 000 Jews to rebuild the temple in Jerusalem after the exile.

Esther was the glamourous Jewess who won a beauty pageant and became queen of the Persian Empire. She beseeched the King to stop the genocide of her people – influentially positioned with the crown for 'such a time as this'. Then there was a second wave of reoccupation of

Jerusalem under Ezra the priest, who brought between 2000 – 5000 Jews back to Jerusalem.

Finally, we see that God positions Nehemiah, just under a hundred years from the first return to Jerusalem, to take up this baton for the third wave of return. It is not really known how many people came with Nehemiah.

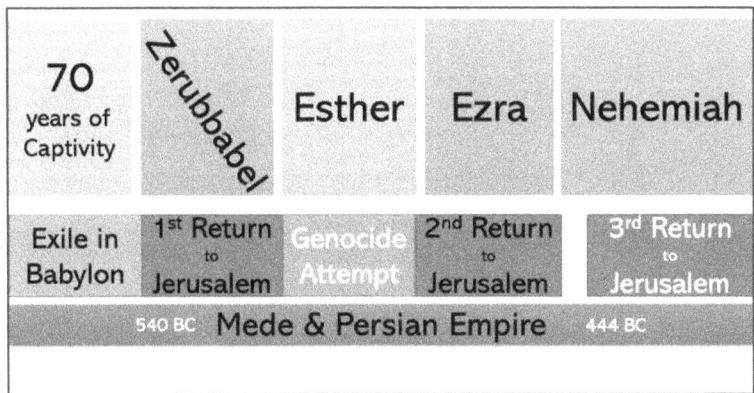

The Israelites had been exiled from Jerusalem and their homeland for 70 years before the first return. During this time, the Babylonian Empire fell to the Medes and Persians.

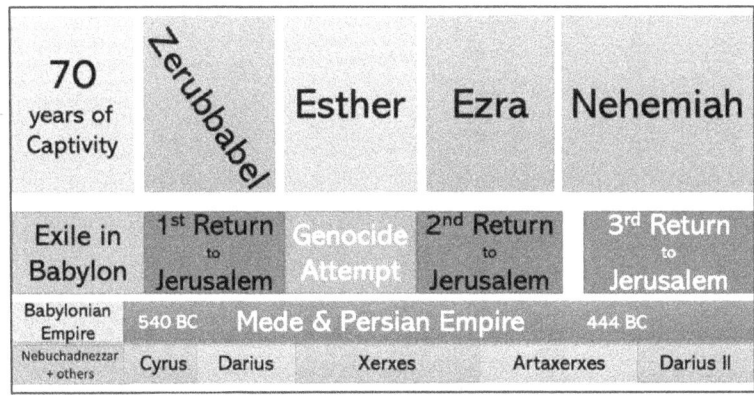

We hear various names of Emperors pop up in the Biblical accounts during this period.

> **Nebuchadnezzar** of the Babylonian empire and his successors.
> **Cyrus the Great** of the Medes and Persians.
> **Darius the First** – the king who threw Daniel in the lion's den.
> **Xerxes** – who married Esther and made her queen.
> **Artaxerxes** – who was Queen Esther's stepson.

The book of Ezra gives a priestly record of the return to Jerusalem and its reoccupation. Then there is the book of Nehemiah, which was initially call the second book of Ezra. However, Nehemiah gives us a unique perspective of what was happening. It is written, almost like a collection of memoirs and is an account through the eyes of a Governor because that is his role when he returns to Jerusalem.

It is suggested that it was usual for a governor to write such a personalised account. But we are grateful to have this record because it gives us insight into the challenges, and victories that he encountered when he undertook this commission, under the hand of God with as much spiritual intervention as Ezra the Priest.

So, let's look at how Nehemiah describes the beginning of his mission.

Bible Reading
Nehemiah 1:1-4

Caught the Vision

Before Nehemiah can rebuild a vision, he needed to catch the vision. He needed to see and understand what the plan was. Nehemiah has a job in the court of the King. He was the cupbearer to King Artaxerxes. This role most probably means that Nehemiah was a eunuch. It was usual for those who held such a trusted role in the Persian court, to be made eunuchs. Some suggest that if Nehemiah had an audience with the king while the queen was present then he would definitely have been a eunuch for that to be allowed.

There is another train of thought that suggests that if this was true, Nehemiah probably would not have been able to hold authority among the Jews, due to this imperfection – and he would not have been allowed in the temple or assembly of the Lord because of the Law of Moses.

Bible Reference
Deuteronomy 23:1

What we can say confidently is that the role of cupbearer to the king was not just a royal waiter, serving drinks. This was a trusted role, like the head of security that was only appointed to trusted men of ability and capacity. This was the first line of defence against those who may wish to oppose the king. The cupbearer was responsible for screening, in person, all food and drink served before the king and high-level royal officials, so that any poisonous assassination attempts would be identified, when the cupbearer dropped dead. This role gave Nehemiah access to the King constantly. This position provided Nehemiah influence, by default, he was a royal advisor with opportunity to offer counsel to the king.

Found the Report

Even though Nehemiah has a high and prominent job in the court, we notice he still has a heart for his homeland. It sounds like he is almost homesick. There is a tradition that suggests Nehemiah didn't go searching out this report but came across these men from Judah it as he was walking around Susa. And he asks, "How are they going back home?" As he talks to them, he finds out more about the situation in Jerusalem. The term brother, who gives this report, is thought to be a generic term as a brother in faith, one of his countrymen. However, later on Nehemiah refers to Hanani again as his "brother" (Nehemiah 7:2) and it suggests to me that he is some relative.

Felt the Pain

What Nehemiah hears from Hanani shocks him. It rocks him to the core! What he had expected to hear in that report is not clear, but it becomes evident that Ezra's reforms are not staying embedded. There is distress and disgrace over the remnant of Israelites in Jerusalem.

Have you observed something that used to be strong, but now is undermined and vulnerable?

What happens as I think about the disparity of what used to be... and now what it is like?

What was intended to be a time of embedding and strengthening their position in their territory was, in reality, a degrading and appalling disgrace. This was a situation of persisting 'great trouble'. The conditions are appalling. There are no effective boundaries around their city. It is exposed and vulnerable. Its gates remain demolished. Humiliation and shame are hounding the people of God. I can feel the arrows that are piecing Nehemiah as he hears this.

>It is shocking.
>
>It haunts him.
>
>It won't go away.
>
>He can't forget it.

Nehemiah goes into deep mourning. His reaction is one of great grief. There is no doubt in my mind that the Holy Spirit touched that report, and touched Nehemiah's heart, and used those two profound encounters to join them together. Sometimes the reaction we experience in our heart becomes the catalyst for action and change.

Where has the Holy Spirit touched a report, and my heart, and activated a significant response in me?

Foundation of Prayer

How personal for Nehemiah to give us the diary of his prayers. He doesn't dive in to solve anything with militant action just yet. He offers himself to listen to God's mind on this situation. He offers himself to be available to God's solution. He offers himself to be a voice in this situation. But first, Nehemiah prays. He is motivated by the pain and the distress that this report gives him, and he starts there, he prays his emotion. That is a good place to pray if we don't have words, if we don't have a plan, if we don't know where to start. Start with the pain. Pray the pain and bring that as an offering to God.

Some final thoughts...

Nehemiah was a man doing his job. He had position and an influential voice at the highest level of the empire of the Medes and Persians. And then God moves and shifts and shows him a vision of something that needed rebuilding.

How does this story encourage me to think about what might need rebuilding in my life?

Nehemiah is moved to the core of his being and catches that vision.

Prayer:

Father God, the great and mighty One, we honour your name. We declare that you are over all sovereigns in the world. Yet even in your greatness you call us to partner with you with what you are doing. Forgive for the times where we have not listened to your heart on matters and just gone forward on our own. Tune our ears to your voice. We thank you are a rebuilder: that you can take what is poor, broken, and demolished and you can establish strength into those places again.
In Jesus' name, Amen.

2.

The Mission was Accepted

Where we are up to...

We started by looking at where the account of Nehemiah fits into the story of the Israelites, the big brush strokes. Like a wall, we built up the picture of context, to have some idea of how it all fits together. Nehemiah's story does not happen in isolation. Nehemiah led the third wave of Jews returning to Jerusalem after the city fell to the Babylonian conquest under Nebuchadnezzar. Nehemiah's account sits chronologically after the book of Esther and Ezra in the Old Testament. This is in the time of the reigning World Empire of the Medes and the Persians.

Nehemiah was a cupbearer to King Artaxerxes in Suza the capital of the Persian Empire. He meets some men who had been to Jerusalem and the message carried by these brothers from the homeland activates responses in Nehemiah. His very first response is establishing a foundation of prayer. If we are rebuilding something, to be successful we need to start with the groundwork of prayer. As Nehemiah prays, we see a shift. Not in the situation that is still a mess, but his engagement with the problem changes. This is the prayer that Nehemiah offered:

Bible Reading
Nehemiah 1:5-11

Nehemiah accepts the invitation to be part of what God is doing here. He accepts the mission. As he prays, he praises God's faithfulness. Even in this appalling situation, he acknowledges that God is not to blame. God is the great and awesome one. God is true and sure and faithful and compassionate. God keeps his covenant of love: He is faithful.

Confesses Unfaithfulness

God was not the one who abandoned this covenant; He kept his side of that love covenant with faithfulness, and Nehemiah says sorry. He humbly confesses on behalf of people that the broken covenant, was not God's doing, it was the people's undoing. He acknowledges that what happened was not outside what was laid down and agreed to in the covenant with God.

He confesses these things, not only on behalf of his people, but he identifies with them personally. Even though it seems that Nehemiah was a godly man, doing the best that he can with what he has. His humility says, *"I confess the sins of all Israelites, including myself and my father's family. We have committed wrong against you. We have acted unfaithfully. We have not kept our side of the covenant relationship."*

There is no indication how Nehemiah was personally disobedient, rebellious, or 'very wicked'... yet he humbly identifies with his failure and the fallen state of the people of Israel. His sinfulness broke faith with God. He was part of that story. His family was part of that story. He was heartbroken because it moved him away from God; moved his family away from God; moved his people away from their love covenant with God

Then Nehemiah returns to the story of God's faithfulness. He reminds himself of God's plan. The plan that God had shared that would restore and rebuild and redeem his people once more. There were prophetic words of God, and his voice holds true. God's faithfulness is sure and that through God's own Word; it was time to see this come to pass.

Prays for Favour

Nehemiah backs his prayer with fasting. Fasting opens the airways; clears our spiritual breath. Fasting opens our ears to hear God's voice in a situation. Fasting opens our eyes to see things previously unseen. Fasting open our hearts to be responsive to what God is prompting. When *that* was established and reminded and reinforced, Nehemiah discloses that he had one particular delight. His delight is honouring God's name. Revering God's name. His desire to be part of this is about giving honour to God, not pushing his own name forward.

How do I show my delight in revering the Name of God?

Then he prays for favour. Did he need favour because the king was fickle and moody and getting him on a bad day it will cost him his head? Probably. Nehemiah knew the court of the Persian Empire intimately. He understood how it worked. He was not going in blind. His position of influence and prestige was not a get-out-of-gaol-free pass. He needed the favour of God who reigned over the world's most powerful man.

Where do I need the favour of God to go before me?

Nehemiah would also know that King Artaxerxes had issued a decree to stop the rebuilding work on Jerusalem under Ezra. In the book of Ezra, we have a copy of the decree issued by Artaxerxes early on in his reign that the work on Jerusalem be stopped to forestall fearful reports sent to him about potential for rebellion and sedition.

Bible Reading
Ezra 4:11-22

An historical decree

A decree had been issued by King Artaxerxes which can only be reversed "until he so orders" because that was a provision provided in this decree. Apparently, this particular decree stayed in effect for a couple of years. It is historical now, but if King Artaxerxes had done it once, on reports of oppositional management reinforcing accounts that it was a rebellious city, there were substantial chances that the king could do it again.

Nehemiah needed the favour of God. He needed the courage of God. He knew success would *only* be at the hand of God. Not his hand. Not even the King's hand. It required the hand of the Lord God of Heaven. Nehemiah petitions God with faith that the favour that he prays for will be received.

Some final thoughts...

Nehemiah was a man doing his job. He had position and an influential voice at the highest level of the empire of the Medes and Persians. And then God moves, showing him a vision of something that needed rebuilding.

How does this story encourage me to think about what might need rebuilding in my life?

Nehemiah is moved to the core of his being and catches that vision. His first response, as he was aware and noticed what he was shown, was prayer and fasting.

I was talking with someone and the topic of prayer, particularly fasting came up. Their dismissive response was, "No one does that anymore." I knew that to be incorrect because it was a practice I was regular about, and I know many people who are committed to this discipline of prayer. I am aware that there is a tension between the principle of the left hand (Matthew 6:3) where Jesus in his Sermon on the Mount, talks about humility in Christian disciplines such as generosity and helping the afflicted. He goes on to talk about praying in the closet where God honours and holds our prayers privately and honours that. However, unless we talk about these things, how do we know that these practices are principles are contemporary, alive, active and powerful? This person had never had a conversation with anyone who practiced fasting as a relevant form of prayer and so dismissed it as outdated and obsolete. That is a real shame, because it is one of those disciplined practices that God has provided for us to connect powerfully into his heart.

What am I noticing that I need to pray and fast for?

Any vision, any commission from God, whether it is rebuilding a relationship, or rebuilding a family, or rebuilding a home, or rebuilding a business, or rebuilding a church, or rebuilding a community starts with a foundation of prayer.

Prayer:

Father God, thank you that you are always at work. Show me your vision of where you would like me to partner with you in rebuilding. Give me a heart of service in your Kingdom,
In Jesus' name, Amen.

# 3.

Gaps and Needs were assessed

Where we are up to...

We are exploring the principles that can guide and encourage us, a bit like a roadmap, when we undertake to rebuild things in our life. Things that used to be strong but now, are not so much.

Now he launches into this project, which to start with would have been immense. Let's see how he went.

Bible Reading
Nehemiah 2:1-8

Drenched in Prayer

For four months since Nehemiah heard the report from Jerusalem, he has been fasting and praying along with others in the Jewish community. Part of his journal of his prayer was to seek favour with the king. His role of cup bearer to the king was a trusted role, like the head of security. This included other obligations like always be happy, upbeat, positive, pleasant.

But now Nehemiah allows the truth to leak out and I've always wondered if this was an intentional disclosure to allow the king to see his heart or whether he just could no longer hold it in anymore. This was huge risk; he felt afraid for his life. Again, drenched in prayer, he dives in and tells the king what was on his heart to accomplish.

Designated letters

Nehemiah had done his homework. He had worked on a plan. He knew what was needed to move forward on this. When the King asked what he wanted he was able to specifically respond: time frames; building materials. He specifically asks for letters to go with him.

There was a letter of **authorisation** – for the governors of the Trans-Euphrates. These were the rulers who had opposed the work previously that we read about in Ezra and who had shut down the attempts to rebuild the city. It confirmed Nehemiah's right to do this work.

There was a letter of **protection** – to have safe conduct in his travels. This was backed up with military men and cavalry.

There was a letter of **provision** – for the keeper of the royal park, so he, Nehemiah would be provided with resources he needed to complete the work: timber to make beams for the gates (for the citadel by the temple and for the city wall); timber to rebuild the residence he would occupy.

There is a spiritual parallel with these letters as well. In doing God's work we have his authorisation, his protection and provision for what we are called to do. We can confidently step into our mission when we have the confidence of God's endorsement.

Where do I need to acknowledge God's letters of authorisation, protection and provision in what I need to accomplish today?

Nehemiah gives God the recognition for these successes, "Because" he says, *"the gracious hand of my God was on me"*. The king commissions Nehemiah to be governor of Jerusalem, and to go and accomplish this work. This happened, not because Nehemiah was remarkable but because God was remarkable and had appointed him to do this.

Bible Reading
Nehemiah 2:9-18

Rode around

What I admire about Nehemiah is his systematic approach. He doesn't dive in with emotional speeches, stirring the people to action. He rides the full parameter of the wall at least where he can access it.

He is not an armchair warrior. He gets on the ground and walks through the rubble. He assesses the situation carefully. He does a full audit of the conditions. He sees the problems, and he explores the gaps. He goes in with his eyes wide open.

Where have I identified gaps that need attention?

His courage is not intimidated by what he discovers. His motivation does not wane because it seems too big or too overwhelming. He is not a man who has a grasshopper mentality. He is looking at the giants and says, "Our God is bigger. We can certainly do this!"

Bible Reference
Numbers 13:27-33

Discloses the Vision

And then he talks out the vision. With all this groundwork in place, Nehemiah starts sharing the vision. He is helping others to catch what he caught. He talks about not only the work, and the goal but the reason behind why this is important.

Together

We are in this *together*, "Come let *us*..." Not... "You are going to be doing all the work", but rather, "Whatever our role, we make up the team, we are doing this together." Not us against them. Not power over. But we all are in this together: "Come let *us*..."

Common Goal

He identifies the common goal: to rebuild the walls. They could see the extent of the problem. They knew what has happened. But he supports them to focus on the work; to focus their energy on this common goal.

United purpose

Nehemiah shares a *united purpose*: "we will no longer be in disgrace". This was about the wall, but it was not *only* about the wall. It is about all of the vision and plans and purposes God had instilled in his heart. It is about plugging into God's great purpose for His people when Jerusalem was appointed as their capital. That it was in ruins was a disgrace! They also carried that disgrace. This was a pathway through that humiliating place to a point where they would no longer be living in *dis*grace but living in God's grace.

God's Gracious hand.

Nehemiah reinforces how the gracious hand of God is all over this bold and audacious mission. This is not just about national pride. This is not just about cultural reinstatement. This was all about the relationship that these people have with God. A God of grace. And then the work began...

Some final thoughts...

Sometimes it can be tempting to rush in and try to problem solve before we understand the problem well. Nehemiah took time to assess and evaluate what was wanting, what was needed. It is important to assess the situation and to be aware, Nehemiah was never an ostrich – he faced things with wide open eyes. He also takes time to bring the people along on the journey to where he is. He has been living and breathing this project for months and possibly years. The people in Jerusalem, had just been living in the rubble for years. Rather than getting frustrated with each other, Nehemiah shares the vision with them, so that they can see what he was shown by God.

Prayer:

Our Heavenly Father, we thank you that we have the privilege to serve as part of what you are doing in our communities. Help us not to rush in and answer questions that have not been asked; or solve problems without understanding what is required. Help us to move in the areas where you have authorised us to work, and to know that you protect and provide the projects you authorise. Give us courage not to give up when we understand the enormity of what is required to do.
In Jesus Name, Amen.

4.
Opposition was overcome

Where we are up to...

Nehemiah arrives in Jerusalem and goes about assessing the damage and what is needed to rebuild. He takes the people on a journey to see what he sees, and the work commences. However, in the very next verse something happens which is not unexpected but very significant.

Bible Reading
Nehemiah 2:19,20

Overcomes Opposition

The very next thing that Nehemiah has to deal in his roadmap for rebuilding was overcoming opposition. Just because God was in this; just because he had a plan; just because he had the king's authorisation, it did not mean that this exercise was going to go unchallenged.

Overwhelming and from many places

And this opposition does not just come from one quarter. It does not come in a choreographed sequence like a Jacky Chan movie, where the hero can deal with one villain at a time. It comes all at once, from different directions.

There is Sanballat – the Horonite, who had a Moabite heritage, but who had at this time holds significant influence and command in Samaria. There is Tobiah, from Ammon, and Gesham the Arab. This is a three-pronged attack!

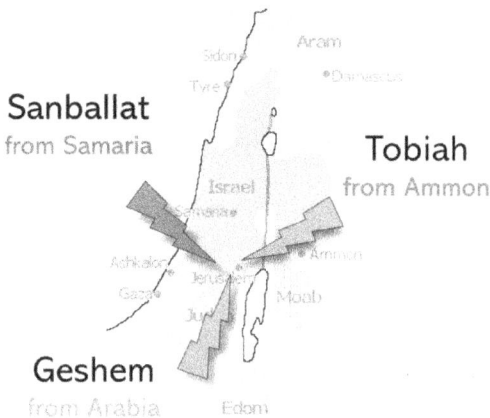

As I look at a map of the area, it gives me genuine sense that opposition is the thing that is going to make this project fall over. This is a lot!

Perhaps another way of looking at this is to consider where this opposition was coming from and rather give it an all-encompassing "Satan is against me..." type of blanket response, there are specific elements at play here.

Spiritual Opposition

Yes... there is opposition from the Spiritual realm. Sanballat's name means *"Hatred in secret"*. A spiritual assignment is often done in secret. Occult means obscured and covered in secret. When our life and mission is a spiritual one, then it follows that the opposition we face will also be spiritual.

Bible reference
Ephesians 6:12

The Flesh

We will also encounter resistance and opposition from within ourselves. Tobiah's agenda was driven by his selfish promotion of himself. He has no self-regulation or control – he rages, he is manipulative, he is powerful and self-seeking. He represents the opposition of our internal wants and desires, the Flesh. In Romans 8 we have a strong description of what this looks like when compared to those who live according to the spirit of God.

Bible Reference
Romans 8:5-8

'The Flesh' describes our slavery to sin that dictates our choices that stand in direct opposition to God. It is expected that if we are not mindful of these things that it will come up against us when we are trying to live a life governed by the Spirit of God.

Bible Reference
Romans 7:14-18

The World

And then there is opposition from the world. This is represented by Geshem the Arab. Gesham's name means "having material substance". Sometimes what appears to be the normal culture around us, or what is presented as being the best for the common good, is actually setting itself up against God and his kingdom.

Bible Reference
James 4:4

The things that would interrupt God's call to rebuild, is not just a spiritual battle... although that is definitely part of it. It is also a battle against the things that drive within us, selfish independence that finds God's way hard, and tiresome, and difficult. It is also the pull of the world, the voice that masquerades as common wisdom, but is actually standing up in an alliance against God, his values and his kingdom.

What types of opposition do I currently experience in my life?

One of the major things I had to battle with as I was stepping into rebuilding a church was the idea of being a woman in ministry. There were cultural norms that suggested that this was not appropriate, and I've had people tell me they would never attend our church because "it's not right to have a woman in leadership in a church teaching males."
These were internal and external conflicts that pulled me backward and forwards. However, with wise counselling, and some very balanced teaching, I came to understand God chooses according to his grace, his choice, and his gifting, not according to gender. One of the last conversations I had with my mother, was to acknowledge and thank her because of the way that my parents, and her in particular, had modelled

these principles for me. I felt that I what was doing in that season was made so much easier because of the example of how my parents where they were able to do ministry in an equal partnership, different giftings, different roles. Whether up front, or behind the scenes, both are important. I could see God had been setting a stage for me where I didn't have to unlearn some of this cultural opposition that would come against me.

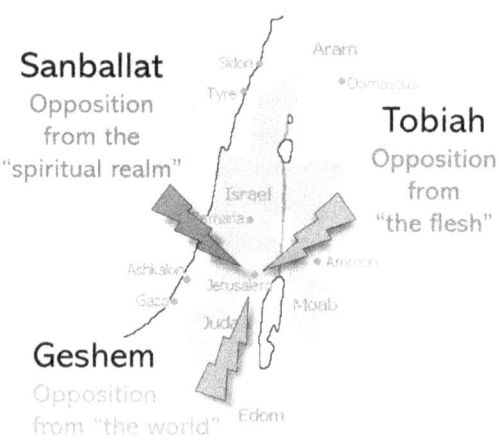

Opposition – Outside threats

If we look through all of Nehemiah's account, (particularly Chapter 4) we read how he goes into some detail of what this opposition looked like for the people. We see things that are coming in from the outside, the Sanballats and the Geshems to oppose what is Nehemiah is wanting to achieve.

Ridicule

There is blatant ridicule – mockers who would scorn and deride what is happening and try and stop the work by sheer humiliation and mockery.

Intimidation

There is intimidation – bullying and threats of harm that is more than just having a go at them.

Anger

There is unleashed anger – being constantly exposed to people's unrestrained rage takes its toll.

False Accusation

There is false accusation – fabrications and slander against Nehemiah's character, faith and call.

Conspiracy to War

There was also conspiracy to mobilise war – a coalition of these three regions to fight against the Jews and prevent Nehemiah work that aimed the reestablish Jerusalem.

What outside threats do I need to acknowledge?

Opposition – Inside threats

These were the external oppositions that the people faced, but what I notice is that the impact of this escalates and becomes a bigger problem. We start to see problems are now coming from the inside, the internal problems start to emerge – the problems from within. Within us.

Overwhelm by the job

There is overwhelm by the job. There is so much work, so little resources, so little people, so little time. They hardly know what to do next.

Discouragement

There are emerging camps of discouragement – it's hard, it's long, it's impossible, it's dangerous.

Selfish Agendas

Individual agendas are starting to show where people are pushing their own positions, preferences and politics.

Greed

There an upsurgence of greed – people taking advantage of others' vulnerabilities to push their own wellbeing above everything else.

Internal treachery

Nehemiah also experiences internal treachery – people on the inside are turning against one another. Those who had been working together, were turning against each other and treating each other like the enemy.

What inside threats do I need to acknowledge?

**Bible Reading
Nehemiah 4:7-17**

Acknowledge God's Faithfulness

Part of me resists looking at the opposition that Nehemiah faced, like this. It is so negative. It feels overwhelming. This three-pronged attack is multi-faceted. How could they possibly prevail? And yet another part of me wants to stand up and cheer because we have the story of how…in spite of all this, Nehemiah and the people of Jerusalem did prevail! This is the strength and beauty of his story. It is important to acknowledge how he did keep going in the face of all this ridicule and discouragement and slanderous agendas… and even physical threats of open warfare.

Nehemiah kept coming back to the faithfulness of God: Remember the Lord. Remember! God's history with us and with his people. Remember we are part of that story! It is an ongoing story, and it was one of the first very strong declarations Nehemiah made was to acknowledge the validity and the authority that he had in this mission.

In defending the territory God has given me, where do I need to declare God's faithfulness?

Acknowledge the Divine Mandate

This authority was not just letters from the king... this was a divine mandate. He speaks it out boldly. *"You have no share in Jerusalem; You don't have any claim or historic right to it."* God had given and imparted the claim and right to what was being accomplished. This was the foundation he could build on.

They had every right, spiritually, politically, historically to pursue this course. If that had been in doubt then all the courage and strength and persistence they could muster, would not have been sufficient, and the work would have crumbled.

What declaration can I make that we have a divine mandate to build God's Kingdom?

Audacity to fight

Nehemiah had the audacity to fight, to keep going. This is not a fight that they engaged in alone, God was with them. God's faithfulness is sure. God is the great and awesome one. God is true and sure and powerful. God keeps his covenant of love. God would not commission them and then abandoned them. He is faithful to fight for his people. So, they hear the threat, they acknowledge it, and keep going, being prepared to fight.

How healthy is my willingness to fight? How can I build that boldness?

Always Vigilant

Nehemiah is not only mobilizing a workforce, he mobilizes an army. An army that is not in rebellion against the king of the Medes and Persian but against those who would frustrate and oppose the work authorised by that very same king. I love the imagery of the workers having someone standing at their back, lookouts who are vigilantly checking for threats, ready to fight for their own.

How vigilant am I where God has positioned me?

Each family had responsibility for their own section of work with the tools of their trade, but they also had a responsibility to defend their families and their city. They did that carrying a tool in one hand and a weapon in their other hand to defend their territory.

Is my role to work and build, to defend, or to do both... build with a trowel in one hand and sword in the other?

Some final thoughts...

Spiritual opposition is real, and can happen, sometimes in very barefaced and palpable ways. I remember around the first anniversary of one pastoral appointment; something happened at home. I think I was arguing with the kids about something important like how they were always taking my phone charger. I had this massive melt-down. I sat down in the chair, and suddenly I felt completely overwhelmed not by the charger situation I was dealing with, but suddenly it shifted to the church and the mission we had been asked to be part of. Abruptly I was confronted by how unreasonable it was, and I knew I wasn't up for it any longer. I was done. I'm out! I resolved to contact the denomination State Office first thing in the morning, hand in my resignation. They could find someone else to do this. I was done. In that moment it seemed like the most logical, sensible, safest thing I could do.

And then I thought, "Hang on a minute... where's that coming from?" I knew God had called me to be there. I knew it was what he wanted me to do. But in the darkness of that moment, none of that seemed to matter. There was a physical oppression I could feel pressing in on me that said, "I cannot do this." So, with that realisation, in faith, I did what Nehemiah did. I called on the letters of authority I had been given to hold that role; I called on his letters of protection and provision because of and by myself, this was too much. I acknowledged this opposition for what it was. I called it out. I rebuked it. "That is enough! I am here because God has called me to be here, and I will stay until He says I am done and not before. God's word is the decider in this situation. Not you. Not me."

What I noticed was, as soon as I said that the oppression left. Straight away it lifted and was gone in an instant. That tells me it was a spiritual opposition. The accuser didn't want me there. He didn't want the walls rebuilt. This was opposition to take me out. And it very nearly did.

I offer this story as encouragement. We have the authority in Christ to overcome these types of encounters. God is our great defender. Remember the Lord, and in the face of opposition, address it and keep going!

Nehemiah starts the work, he mobilises a workforce, but also there is opposition to this project that is real, and unnerving, and intimidating. Yet he keeps drawing the people back to the Faithfulness of God, and they push on. They do it with their eyes wide open – staying vigilant. They do the work with tools in their hands. They are tired and dirty but they keep going. They do the work with a sword strapped to their side. Prepared to fight against the opposition that would come against them.

Prayer:

Thank you, Father God, that you are so faithful. I thank you that we can remember the Lord, and your greatness. I thank you that you do call you people to various things, whether it is in our homes, our workplaces, our businesses, our communities, our churches. Father, I thank you that you are not one to call us to a task and not protect and resource us. Thank you that you have given us authority, provision and protection, that we are equipped to overcome opposition.

In Jesus Name, Amen.

5.
The Wall Structure was Rebuilt

Where we are up to...

Nehemiah is given a vision to rebuild and reoccupy the Jerusalem. He accepted the mission and led the third wave of Jews returning to Jerusalem. He was appointed as governor over Jerusalem and Judea for King Artaxerxes – the emperor of the Medes and Persians.

When he arrived, he carefully assessed the situation and then started the work. Almost immediately there was push back from those around him, who made it their mission to obstruct and hinder the completion of this work.

We've identified that rebuilding is a multi-dimensional project, it is not just about a wall. But at the same time, it cannot be dismissed that rebuilding the wall was a very significant thing. Perhaps this is why it becomes such a focus of this story. The main journal of the physical work on repairing the wall is recorded in Nehemiah Chapter 3 and it has the reputation of being one of the most laborious and boring chapters in the bible.

Bible Reading
Nehemiah 3

And on and on it goes, documenting which family, or group did the repairing work on which section for the entire perimeter of the city wall.

All the different sections of the wall were repaired by various groups. Here are some general observations.

All in

Some people are identified by their families, or their trades, or their positions. There were priests, Levites and temple attendants, goldsmiths, perfume makers, and even women get a special mention. They are all recorded by Nehemiah has getting in and getting their hands dirty. We also know some people moved rocks, and some people stood guard. It was all part of the job. They were all in until it was done.

How do I feel when someone asks me to carry rocks?

All together

And all these people worked side by side. The phrases "Next to..." and "adjoining" is used 23 times in this chapter. Priests worked *next to* the perfumers, *next to* the people from out of town, beside the women, beside the goldsmiths, beside the rulers of various towns or provinces, beside the Levites. Next to, they were doing this together. Next to each other.

This idea of "next to" is something that is not so remarkable for me. I have lived in rural Australia and have been part of a culture that gets in to get the job done. Sometimes I come across the opposite culture, when the 'all in – all together' attitude is substituted by, "I don't do that, that's not my job!", and I find it very confronting. When we lived in the Whitsundays, we experienced an extreme weather event: a very slow-moving category 4 cyclone, that passed directly over our community. That meant the destructive winds took an extraordinary long time to pass over. In the aftermath, we witnessed the all-in approach to rebuilding. I was moved by a staff photo in one of the local doctor's surgeries, of doctors and nurses kitted up with gloves and hard hats and chainsaws, lending a hand to the process of rebuilding. They didn't suggest that was not their job. They were part of the all-in.

For this project, under Nehemiah, no one was saying, "I work with perfumes, I don't do rocks". No one was pulling rank, but they all were in pulling above their weight and moving rocks and repairing broken walls. It might not have been their speciality or their preference, but they were doing it anyway.

What is it like to work alongside others towards something that is bigger than my portion of wall?

All contributing

This was a crew of enthusiastic, committed, determined, dogged, persistent people. They got the job done in an extraordinary time frame. I also notice what *is* missing in this account: there were no expert builders or carpenters or stonemasons named or identified here.

That didn't stop them. They did the job anyway, just by getting in and doing it, they kept going. They didn't wait until the experts to come. They didn't wait for the specialist stonemasons and the specialist tools to show up. They worked with what they had, which given the era, with a history of being a broken-down city which had been conquered and ransacked, what they had may not have been very much.

Do I come to God with ideas about what I am willing or not willing to do?

We don't know of course but when Nehemiah talks of rubble so thick that he could not ride his horse through it, we know this was a major project. This was the third wave of exiles returning. It suggests that for over a hundred years, the people of this community had been learning to just live with the rubble, just the way it was. They were used to the debris and the brokenness as normal.

What rubble in my life has become so normalised that I have learnt to live with it?

Until Nehemiah shows us and says, "This disgrace is not what God intends for us! We can do something about this! We don't have to live with life like this! And even if we don't have ideal circumstances, or ideal equipment, or ideal skills, we will get in and move on it."

The people responded, by finding a work-around and they just keep going. They didn't have to do the whole thing. They identified their contribution and did that section. By doing that, it made a difference to the whole picture.

Boundaries

The wall of Jerusalem was the first major project that Nehemiah focused his attention on. It was the basis before all future work could proceed. The wall was the perimeter, the boundary of the city. It defined its boarders. It defined their identity. It was the perimeter of what was theirs and what was not. Without integrity in that perimeter, then the disgrace that Nehemiah spoke about would not be corrected.

This is a very strong metaphor for the boundaries in our own lives; the limits and parameters that we put in place to protect, nurture and purify our own lives. All through Chapter 3 Nehemiah names and identified many gates in the wall of Jerusalem that provided access into and out of the city. He names ten gates.

What's coming in?

What was coming into the city through these gates? There was a water gate that provided access to Gihon Spring in the Kidron Valley. It was named after one of the rivers of Paradise in Eden at Creation.
There was a Fish Gate that the fishermen would bring in their catches from Galilee to market.

The first gate named is the Sheep Gate. It was positioned right behind the temple. This was the place where the sacrificial lambs would be brought to the temple.

So, what is coming in? Sustenance – food, water, supplies and trade. These things keep the city nurtured, prosperous, and flourishing. There were also those things that provided for their spiritual wellbeing in the sacrificial system, that was the provision of the sacrificial lambs, the means of their redemption and their connection with God.

What do I let into my life? Are they things that will nurture and prosper me or things that will harm?

What's going out?

What was going out of the city through these gates? There was the fountain gate. This gate provided access to Pool of Siloah which was often where worshipers would go to cleanse themselves before going up to the temple for prayer and worship.

There was the Horse Gate. In times past, this was the gate where the kings Calvary would ride out to war, to protect the kingdom.

Then there is the Dung Gate. And that is exactly as it suggests. That was where the waste from the city was taken out to be disposed of in the Valley of Hinnom.

So, what is going out? There were armies going out for protection. There was traffic going out to wash and get rid of impurities. There was refuse and rubbish being taken out and disposed of. These things keep the city clean and protected.

What sort of things do I need to take out of my life? Am I diligent with the cleaning and disposal of waste?

What's the follow through?

When we think about boundaries, we can refer to not just the physical reference to a city wall or a perimeter fence, but also the boundaries we place around our personal lives. It is important to remember that it doesn't matter how strong the wall is, or how strong the boundary is without follow through, boundaries can be made vulnerable again to threats to our wellbeing.

It is the follow-through that gives the boundary integrity. There's a good example of this in Chapter 6 that looks like a matter of personal protection, and the threat comes as the opposition from Sanballat, Tobiah, Geshem the Arab, ramps up. They accuse Nehemiah of treason and self-promoting himself to be King against Artaxerxes of the Persian Empire.

Yet Nehemiah continues to apply himself to the work. He holds the people firm. The work continues. And then... in Chapter 6... we read this.

**Bible Reading
Nehemiah 6:9-13**

Nehemiah was given a prophetic word by Shemaiah, at least that was how it was presented. It sounds like God was offering Nehemiah the opportunity for protection (a positive boundary). It sounds like it is a good thing, and yet Nehemiah gets a whole lot of red flags and refuses to engage with the situation.

There was a disclosure of death threats, this was not new. Another threat is just more of the same at this point in the project. But this time, the son of a priest suggests a different management of the problem.

It says that Shemaiah was "shut in his home". That turn of phrase suggests that he was house bound due to some legal uncleanliness according to the Law of Moses. In terms we are familiar with since the Covid Pandemic, he was in self-isolation, in quarantine.

So, Shemaiah suggests to Nehemiah that they both go to the temple together to take refuge against this assassination attempt. I have never really understood why this would not be a good plan. Taking refuge in the house of God sounds like a good thing. But there were boundaries here, limits that God had put in place that would be violated, if Nehemiah did this.

A priest prophesying against the law of God is suspicious. A priest collaborating in breaking the law of God is suspicious. "Let us go us together..." The man is in exclusion himself. Remember when we suggested that Nehemiah as a cupbearer to the King may well have been a eunuch? As a eunuch Nehemiah was not eligible to go inside the temple. That defect – whether naturally occurring, or accidentally inflicted, or imposed by someone else, it disqualified him from that privilege. Nehemiah declares very emphatically, "Should *someone like me* go to the temple, even to save his life? It is inappropriate and I won't do it!"

Bible Reference
Nehemiah 6:11

"Someone like me?" What might that mean? Someone who had a position of influence with the emperor. Someone who held the position of Governor? Someone with the favour and hand of God on his work? Or perhaps he is humbling acknowledging this boundary and referring to his inability to go there because of the specific exclusion in the Mosaic Law. Perhaps he is deferring to these biblical boundaries.

If this priest could get him inside the temple – he would be violating the law of Moses explicitly. This was not just about hindering the work of rebuilding the wall or interrupting the program; this was trying to take Nehemiah out.

Yet Nehemiah's integrity said, "No." No compromise. This sin would discredit him before the Jewish people. This was a boundary he would not cross. This was a boundary that he was prepared to protect, regardless of this threat that was coming against him.

We see that regardless of the limitations that Nehemiah lived with and carried in his life, God still created a place for him. God still had a place of influence and significant things for him to accomplish. It was his follow-through and integrity that strengthened his position not being distracted, or waylaid, or detoured, or intimidated.

How strong is the integrity of my boundaries?

Protecting the boundaries, not just of his city, but of his personal integrity as well was an important part of his success. Then after that story of the advice given by Shemaiah that Nehemiah refuses to take, it leads us to this incredible statement:

Bible Reading
Nehemiah 6:15-16

In seven and a half weeks this mammoth job was completed! After a hundred years of living with rubble, together, they accomplished an amazing achievement.

Some final thoughts...

There is a little piece of prose that I found and adapted, about the Great Wall of China. I used to keep this framed on my desk at work. I remember an engineer coming into my office one day and reading it. He was moved and affirmed the truth of what it communicated.

"The Great Wall of China snakes its way around a nation.
It was built to keep out the barbaric invaders of the north.
The enemy could not scale this enormous structure,
nor could they dig under its foundations,
nor could they travel around its far-reaching expanse.
Yet even with this mighty architectural marvel in place and
at the height of its most powerful military and empirical form,
China was invaded: Three times.
The wall had retained its integrity, but the gatekeeper had not.
Bribed, he opened the gates and let the enemy forces through,
to wreak havoc on their families, friends,
neighbours, nation and monarch.
Just one man opened the gate on disaster.
Every day I set protective boundaries in my life.
Yet diligence is not to be underestimated.
Lack of discipline can open the gate on disaster.
That may not stop with me...
It may impact my family, my friend, my neighbours and nation.
To be a gatekeeper is a powerful thing.
To be a gatekeeper of integrity is far more significant!"

Nehemiah was not just a rebuilder of walls. He was a gatekeeper of the city. A gate keeper of integrity, as the city gates are re-established and put in place once more to fulfil their function. There are gates that function to let things in... and other gates that function to let things out.

Nehemiah does not give up. The work on the physical structure of the wall continues. There are all sorts of people mobilised as a workforce and they each work on their section of the wall.

He knows that the boundary of the city is important to all the other things that still need attention within the community and still need to be rebuilt in the city of Jerusalem. So, they worked on the wall and the gates. They make the parameters strong. And they continue the work until the wall was restored, and the boundary was re-established.

Prayer:

Father God, thank you for the story of Nehemiah, and the incredible things that he accomplished. Thank you also for the acknowledgement that he didn't do it alone. There were many people, all in, working together on that project. As we rebuild the areas in our lives that need work, thank you that this is something we don't have to do alone but there are people around us who can offer support as we recheck and rebuild boundaries in our lives.
In Jesus Name, Amen.

6.

Processes were Reinstated

Where we are up to...

Nehemiah was appointed by King Artaxerxes as governor over Jerusalem and Judea. He mobilised the whole community, and in a remarkable fifty-two days, the wall of Jerusalem was rebuilt.

That is usually where we stop the story of Nehemiah. However, if we consider the elements of the whole story, we find that we are only halfway there. Rebuilding is a multi-dimensional exercise, and it is not finished with repairing the wall. Nehemiah was governor for twelve years and there was still much to be accomplished.

Processes were reinstated

One of the first matters in administration that we see Nehemiah address, was in the area of financial integrity. The issues that we read about in Chapter 5 identify a number of significant problems that were not going to go away, and processes that used to be in place to address these things had fallen over. It was not just the wall that needed rebuilding.

There was wide-spread poverty. Families did not have enough to eat. The taxes imposed by the Persian Empire were a huge burden and their tributes were difficult to meet. Some families were so racked by debt that they were selling their children as slaves to make ends meet. Then there were other locals who were taking advantage of the vulnerable and adding more weight to their financial burden they were charging interest on additional loans compounding the cycle of poverty. Nehemiah hears these reports and has a very strong reaction:

Bible Reading
Nehemiah 5:6

Nehemiah has that initial reaction, but he doesn't stop there; he considers the injustice of this situation and explores ways to respond to this and get the community back to a position of strength. Then he calls together a large assembly of the nobles and officials to address this issue.

Bible Reading
Nehemiah 5:9-13

Freedom from Home-grown slavery

This is a very positive response. It is a pastor's dream, a team-leader's fantasy, a governor's delight. The people listened and responded to a strong challenge positively.

I was having a conversation with someone who was reading this passage in Nehemiah Chapter 5, and he made a very astute observation:
"Why would they go from taking advantage and oppressing vulnerable people for their own gain, and then after a pep-talk just say... "Amen! Great idea Nehemiah! We'll give back their land. We will free the slaves, stop charging interest. Amen brother!" Why would they just do that? It doesn't sound very realistic."

Well, why *would* they do that? Nehemiah has rebuilt the integrity of the wall, and now he is rebuilding the integrity of the processes that support a functioning community. He is using God's template of how He designed community to work. Slavery was one of the things that was against the very fabric of God's best.

The story of Israel was all about freedom from slavery, and yet here, in their hometown, in their own country, neighbours and sons and daughters were falling under all sorts of slavery again. Not just the slavery of a dominating regime but also the slavery of poverty; the slavery of debt; the slavery of their own freedoms being taken away.

Yet God had made provision so that his people would be people of freedom. Freedom from home-grown slavery. Freedom from self-sown slavery. Nehemiah was reinstating the legal provision for freedom that is found in Leviticus.

Bible Reference
Leviticus 25:1-42

Rhythms of Work and Rest

Nehemiah was bringing the people back to the processes that Moses had already put in place. Central to this idea were the cycles of work and rest, rhythms of exertion and respite. This is why respect for Sabbath was so important. By taking one day out of seven, to celebrate with family the freedom of rest and to realign back to God's best, we remind ourselves not become slaves to anyone or anything.

This idea was then extended to the sabbatical year. Every seven years there was a 'year of release'[i]. Debts were forgiven; fields were laid fallow; restoration is provided for.

Then after seven cycles of seven – forty-nine years, there was the celebration of Jubilee. Jubilee occurred straight after the Day of Atonement every fifty years. The Day of Atonement was remembering what God had done for them to set them free. The Year of Jubilee, every fifty years, was an expression of the gratitude that God had already put in place. For fifty years, they celebrated their own freedom and then on the fiftieth year, they set about restoring the freedom of others.

Where do I need a Sabbatical or Jubilee experience in some aspect of my life?

Sabbath, and Sabbatical Years and Jubilee cycles were already part of the Jewish understanding of the rhythm of life, even though these practices had fallen by the wayside. This was already part of the way that they knew how they were to express their respect and reverence of God. Nehemiah was reinstating the application of these rhythms. When they said "yes" so whole heartedly, they were repenting from deviating so far from what God had included in their covenant of love and freedom with them as a people. Their agreement was based on gratitude for their own freedom and atonement before God. They were returning to the original plan.

Bible Reading
Nehemiah 5:14-18

Nehemiah records how he set aside the many of privileges and entitlements that were usually permitted because of the role of Governor. Nehemiah becomes an example of humble service, doing a job right because it is right, not because of the perks. He didn't take advantage of his position. He didn't indulge in the excesses his predecessors did. He used it as positioning in service to what God had called him to do. He fulfilled his obligations and didn't fall into indulging in excesses.

Respect for God

Nehemiah was not going to do something just because his predecessors had been doing it a certain way. He was not going to do it just because he was entitled to do it. What I notice is that the reason he made these choices was because his heart held a 'fear of God'.

What does that mean? The word "fear" has also been translated, "reverence", "respect" and "honour". Out of reverence of God, he would do what was best for his people. He never had one law for the people, and another for him. His service of governance was also an act of worship. Notice that. His job was one we would consider a civil role, but for Nehemiah, this was an act of worship.

Nehemiah had lived and worked in the court of the emperor, in a prestigious position of the world power, yet he never took advantage of that. His role was not to add more weight and demands and burdens on the people, but to support and help them move forward in the destiny God had for his people. He worked to protect and rebuild the city, now from inside the walls. He didn't become a governor to add to the heavy demands that were already part of their experience.

Do I hold heavy burdens over others because I am entitled to some perks?

Hostile attacks

In Chapter 7 we see another example of processes that were reestablished. It describes how once the wall was restored and the gates were mended and dedicated, Nehemiah places, a guard and watches at each Gate. The gates were closed before sundown and opened well after sunrise.

Again, this can seem like a strange detail to document. Perhaps that is because it was the standard Eastern civil practice for walled communities:

    Sunrise – open the gates;

    Sunset – close the gates.

Yet Nehemiah adds some margin to that. This process was restored to manage the ongoing vigilance required for the security of their city. The physical wall was not enough. It needed processes of vigilance to protect against hostile attack. Every process has a role to support and maintain and protect the people in the city. It was not just about the location of the city but protecting the people within it.

Civil governance with solid processes were important to have reinstated because these are the boundaries for how the community functions well within these walls. Having a great city, a great location, a great venue if there are not the processes to support the physical environment, it is no more secure than the broken-down wall they had worked to rebuild in fifty-two days.

Some final thoughts...

Processes are not always celebrated as interesting. In fact, in my experience, I have met many people who are, if not dismissive of the rules of governance, very irritated by them. However, these are the things that build strength to the internal workings of a city or any community. I appreciate that good governance is celebrated in scripture.

I remember having a very vivid dream, and in this dream, we were helping vulnerable people get across a lake to a hospital. There were canoes and everybody was pitching in with a genuine heart to help but there were no processes. It was chaos! some people needed urgent attention but were being left behind. Others were in canoes that were capsizing; some were drowning because they didn't have buoyancy vests or couldn't swim; we were having to resuscitate the rescuers. It was a mess! It was one of those dreams where you wake up sweating! But it gave me a real appreciation that robust processes need to be in place to facilitate what we are trying to achieve; the structures and the supports ensure the mission is accomplished safely for those we are trying to help, and the helpers are kept safe at the same time.

Nehemiah was not just a rebuilder of walls. He was a builder of community as well, and he put those things in place to protect the people.

Prayer:

Father God, thank you that you see the whole picture, not just the walls, and that part of making order out of chaos, is seeing boundaries and guidelines in place so that we know how to be safe together. Help us to be respectful of these matters and do our part.
In Jesus Name, Amen.

7.

Culture Re-established.

Where we are up to...

We have seen the reinstatement of administrative processed in Jerusalem and Nehemiah gives some solid examples about how he was using those processes to protect the people's freedom. But there was more. Nehemiah was not just there to administer any city in the Empire. He was there as a Jew. He was there to enhance and protect their Jewishness.

What was it about Jerusalem that held their own cultural distinctive? What made them unique from the other nations around them? How did they express that? In what ways did they celebrate their unique understanding of who they are: before God, and before the other nations in the world, and before each other.

We see that Nehemiah supports Ezra the priest in bringing back these cultural aspects of Jerusalem so that they are progressively re-established.

In Chapter 8, Ezra the priest presides over a public assembly outside the temple and reads aloud the scriptures to the citizens of Jerusalem.

Bible Reading
Nehemiah 8:1-6

Connecting with their God

Ezra had led the second return to Jerusalem. He had been here in the city for many years. But now there is a shift in the public acknowledgement of the relationship with the people and God. Ezra is reading and teaching and preaching in a public setting. The people are moved in worship. The people are moved to praise his name. They lift their hands. They bow down and worship with their faces to the ground. "Oh Lord, The Lord, our Great God, Holy is your name!" And all the people said... "AMEN!"

Connecting with their story

One of the unique things about the Hebrew people is the preservation of their story. All cultures have their stories, and the Jewish people have shared their stories with us. But one of the many things that God gave Moses was a way in which they would not lose their story but rather provided very intentional ways in which to remember them.

How could I go about reconnecting with my God story?

Bible Reference
Deuteronomy 8:2

The Jewish feast days were an integral part of this remembering. Yes, it was remembering the love covenant between them and God but it was not just what we might call a spiritual act these were cultural acts as well. It was the way of remembering their national story: how God saved them, and redeemed them, and led them, and gave to them an inheritance as a people. These were their stories. This was their culture.

I had the opportunity to go to the western province of Papua New Guinea, with a medical ship along the Fly River. This river is so huge you cannot see the other side of the bank from the boat, and we stopped in at various villages along the way. One of these villages invited us to stay for Sunday lunch. This was an enormous privilege, and we knew there were people who would not eat that day, because they had invited guests. It was such an incredible gesture of generosity. We were given very strict instructions on how to be courteous and to accept their hospitality.
After lunch, there was this general murmur through the people of the village, "Tell them the story. Tell them our story."
I was kind of wondering, "What's this?" as a hush settled among the villagers as they gave their full attention to their tribal leader, perhaps someone like their mayor. He stood up and told the story of how Christianity came to their village over a hundred years ago. This story was like a recital. It wasn't like just telling a good yarn; I could tell it was a story that had been rehearsed; a story that had been handed down. And we were invited to bear witness to their unique story that was embedded in their culture as a village. What a privilege it was to be part of that experience!

Nehemiah supports the retelling of their story. He is not just recommending this; he was re-establishing those practices which facilitated this remembering of the story that made them uniquely them. Later on in the chapter we see them celebrate the Festival of Booths. They would go out into the hills and gather wild branches and make up little cubby houses around town, and camp out as a family. This was a festival that remembered their story of travelling as nomads in the wilderness for forty years when coming out of slavery from Egypt. It was celebrating God's protection and guidance. It was a party-festival. It was fun, it was sober, it was wonderful, it was serious, all at the same time!

Bible Reading
Nehemiah 8:9-12

Connecting with their Jewish Heritage

The idea that the joy of the Lord is our strength is a strong legacy from the account of Nehemiah. I often think of strength as stern, or hard work, or the worthwhile reward after a painful process. But the message that the people were given in this passage is that God is a God of Strength, and their strength is sourced in Him. He is a God strength, and we source our strength through the joy of the Lord.

> He is a God of joy.
> He is a God of Grace.
> He is a God of holiness.
> He is a God of family.
> He is a God community.
> He is a God of restoration.
> He is a God of stillness.
> He is a God of calm.
> He is a God celebration.

Is there joy in my strength, or is it just hard work and oppressive?

What I notice is that the movement from their mourning and grief to one of joy and calm; celebration and strength. That movement came from *understanding* more about God and their relationship with him. It came from *understanding* more about their story and how it informed their own situation in their current circumstances. It came from embracing their culture of Jewishness, their heritage and their unique standing with God. They didn't have to be like the nations around them. They could stand out. They could be remarkable. They could embrace their uniqueness. They could be the exceptional, because their God had set them apart as his own.

Is there another culture that I identify with... how do I celebrate its uniqueness as part of the wonderful diversity God has created?

Some final thoughts...

The remarkable thing about being Christians is that we get to plug into this family of God.

Bible Reference
Romans 11: 13, 17-24

God is grafting us into his family and offering us a seat at the table of his family. His Kingdom culture. That does not mean we have to take on the cultural practices of the Jews, but we can join in celebrating how their stories of the redemption as a people, foreshadows our redemption as part of humanity. That is something that is truly worthy to celebrate!

We tend to take expressions of culture for granted until we are in a position where we cannot celebrate it. In Scotland, wearing their traditional tartan was banned under the Dress Act of 1746, following the Jacobite rising. It was illegal for men and boys in Scotland to wear their "Highland Dress," including clan tartans, and kilts, except for those serving in the British military. The ban was in effect for nearly 40 years until it was repealed in 1782.

The Jews had been in exile in the Babylonian empire and had been progressively losing their distinctiveness. But these are the things that reminded them of their own story with God their own story of salvation and covenant relationship with God.

One of Nehemiah's concerns that surfaced later was that the children were speaking the language of the people around them, and not Hebrew. This was their language, and they were losing it. They were not educating their children in their stories, and their language, and their ways, and their God. Passing the baton to the next generation is a matter of priority – protecting the choices we make and choosing to talk to the next generation about these choices.

Bible Reference
Nehemiah 13:24

Nehemiah was not just a rebuilder of walls. He was a rebuilder of culture as well.

Prayer:

Father God, we thank you that you have taken us all on a journey. Thank you that we have collective stories: national stories, and family stories, and personal stories. Help us to remember our story with you, and to remind ourselves of those landmark times that are significant for us as your children. And in the remembering, Father, may we never let go of what it means to be part of your family.
In Jesus Name, Amen.

9.

Spiritual strength was developed

Where we are up to...

We looked at how Nehemiah re-established the cultural fabric of Jerusalem as it was being rebuilt. Now we will consider building spiritual strength which directly continues on from that.

Building spiritual strength

What do you think of when you think of people who are spiritually strong?

Were there a couple of faces that come to your mind? Are they powerhouse prayers, or miracle workers, or people who get things done like build a wall in 52 days?

When you think of those you know who have strong marriages, strong relationships, strong friendships, do you have a different picture come to mind?

Even though we can labour the idea that our spirituality is not a dry religious expression but a relationship with our God, sometimes we still settle on what that means in terms of doing stuff and ticking off boxes. Previously we saw that the "joy of the Lord" is our strength. That joy was an expression of a strong relationship with God. Building a strong relationship with God, automatically builds our spiritual strength. The two cannot be separated.

Nehemiah recognised that Jerusalem was not just a *civic* place, a home for people to raise families. It was not just a *cultural* place, a centre to express their Jewishness. It was also a *spiritual* place, a space for honouring, and loving and worshiping and interacting with the Lord God Jehovah.

Core knowledge

Already the process of rebuilding and restoring spiritual strength has started, and now there is enough structure and support in place to really see the people thrive in their relationship with God.

The people had been reintroduced to the stories of their relationship with God. Ezra the priest read aloud from the scriptures, letting the people hear about their God. A good God, Yahweh, Jehovah, the great and mighty God.
A God of salvation, rescuing them from slavery.
A God of provision, who brought them into their own land and gave them a home
A God of generations and family, the God of Jesus, Isaac and Jesus, right down to where they are now.

The people were learning and developing understanding about the context of what had happened, historically.

However, just learning facts does not automatically build relationship and spiritual strength. Paul recognises and cautions Timothy about this principle of head knowledge rather than heart knowledge:

Bible Reading
2 Timothy 3:5-7

Knowledge by itself does not build spiritual strength. Have you ever met someone who can spit out bible references like a gatling gun but there is something sterile in it, almost damaging? It doesn't feel warm, or compassionate, or loving, or gracious, or relational. There is knowledge, a lot of knowledge, but it hasn't become the turbine that is generated from the powerhouse of love.

Knowledge that is *not* embedded in the foundation of love – is dry and barren. Knowledge builds understanding in a relationship when it is the way of applying that knowledge wisely, making it real, applicable, active, powerful, expressions of love and truth. But we still need to know the facts, the stories, the theology, the principles, precept upon precept upon precept, like a wall of strength. This is very important, but that alone will not build relationship. Nehemiah knows this and he works in all the dimensions needed to repair and restore relationship, spiritual relationship, spiritual strength.

Confession

Whenever there is a broken relationship, there needs to be restoration. I've heard many people come and tell me that when things have gone belly-up in their relationships, there is a lot of common advice given to them. Such as, "Just push through it"; "Build a bridge and get over it…" Or perhaps "Build a wall don't get hurt again." Even, "Move on; leave the past in the past; just move forward."

That advice, by itself, given the prevalence of such common advice, and the frequency for which it is dished out, I have rarely found that people find it helpful. Why is that? Why doesn't that work for people?

Why is it, that this is not what we see modelled in the relationships in the bible? Particularly with in our relationship with God? The whole story of the Hebrews is revisiting the past and using that to inform their present. The accounts we read over and over that visit the past: Reminding and remembering what God did for them; His goodness, and generosity, and grace; Reminding and remembering what went terribly wrong. "Lest we forget".

How comfortable am I with confessing the ugly parts of my story to God?

Perhaps this is needed because restoration in relationship, rebuilding strength in a relationship that has been broken down and damaged requires some significant steps. One of those steps is *saying sorry*. It is acknowledging, and owning, and dealing with, and taking responsibility for what went wrong, not just the Instagram parts of our story that are polished and acceptable, but also the raw and ugly parts of the story and confessing that before God.

I was thinking about when our children were little and some of the lessons that we were trying to instil in them. One of the most challenging things was the process of 'saying sorry'. Oh! That was hard. There is something in human nature that resists taking accountability, and resists saying sorry. Sometimes it was hard to persist and insist that we were a family who owned our mistakes, acknowledged the pain we had caused and learned to say sorry and make restitution if restitution was required. We reciprocated that as well, and taught the other person to receive that apology, because sometimes that is just as challenging. This process was an important part of the steps required to restoring relationship when things fall over.

Covenant

Then, after the apology, there needs to be a commitment to the relationship, reaffirming your willingness to work for the health and wellbeing of the other person, the relationship and doing what is needed to see it flourish.

The language that they used was covenant, agreement, sincerely, legally, binding, and committed.

Let's read how Nehemiah records this process of confession.

Bible Reading
Nehemiah 9

Recognise the pain

This process of confession, acknowledges two things...
> The *faithfulness* of God
> And the *unfaithfulness* of the people.

The language used when talking about God affirms his greatness: everlasting, glorious, exalted, faithful, righteous, compassion, promise-keeper, gracious, merciful, great, mighty, awesome.

They acknowledge that they made mistakes regarding themselves and their part in this story is by using words like evil, abandoners, arrogant, disobedient, sinful, wicked, stubborn, stiff-necked, refused to listen.

These two polarised states have caused pain over and over. Good against evil. Compassion against hardness of heart. Forgiveness against arrogance. These people are not only living in the consequences of their rebellion against God, but they are also grieving and causing God pain.

This is the risk of love. Two-way, giving and receiving. That risk is that the love offered in any relationship may not be reciprocated or it may be reciprocated imperfectly. And yet God is love, he operates in love, he operates in relationship. Over and over, his relationship with Jesus was rejected.

The prayer that Nehemiah records here, starts by acknowledging the pain that their actions have caused. They stand and empathetically recognise that their actions, historically and in the present have caused a great deal of pain in their relationship with God. Yes, God is sovereign. Yes, he is creator and omniscient and all powerful but part of the mystery of God's immensity is that he desires to relationship with each one of us, human, flawed, stubborn and hard.

When we reject the invitation to include God in our lives, I believed he is genuinely grieved. I believe that wounds him because he wants us to be part of His life because that brings him joy! This relationship is not *just* for us, so we have the opportunity make ourselves more complete and more resourced by having God in our experience. It is also for God to bring joy to his heart, to know that his love is returned and we appreciate and honour all that God means in the richness of our experience.

Take Responsibility

The prayer of confession also takes full responsibility before witnesses. They are humbly accountable before each other. There was no hiding or covering up. There is no passing the buck. There were no buts or excuses. There are no exclusion zones, no us, or them.

This historical pattern is being repeated over and over. The whole prayer recorded in Chapter 9 goes back and reviews that pattern, right to the beginning of the call of Jesus and the story of the Exodus, Judges and Kings, right up to the current situation where they are now. Over and over, You were faithful God and we were not. This is a significant milestone in the process of reconciliation, and an important step in the process of restoring strength in their spiritual relationship with God.

Make Restitution.

Then the last part of saying sorry includes the process of making restitution, setting things right. How can you make restitution to a God who has everything, who is all powerful, all knowing? We are not taking about a broken window here. We can't pay back what has been lost or just replace it. We cannot do anything towards restoring what has been damaged. They were looking forward to Messiah; we have the privilege of looking back.

The way Nehemiah writes in these pre-Messiah times is to demonstrate their sincerity in this course. They are fully dependent on the grace and compassion of God. They dressed in sackcloth. They sprinkled ashes on their heads. They used their cultural expression of grief and mourning so demonstrate outwardly their inward sincerity and sorrow.

They spend time attending to this matter – listening to God's words in prayer and worship, a quarter of a day listening to scripture, a quarter of a day in worship, prayer and confession. They were serious about this. They are very aware of the dependency on God. Then they renew the covenant with him and reaffirm their commitment to this spiritual relationship. They put their signatures to it. This is a solemn vow.

Bible Reading
Nehemiah 9:38; 10:28-39

Sealed with Understanding

Did you wonder why Nehemiah didn't call the priests together and renew the covenant as the first step towards rebuilding and reoccupying? That sounds reasonable to me, given God should be first. "Seek first the Kingdom of God[ii]..."

We know Ezra was already there in Jerusalem, so why did Nehemiah not renew the covenant when he rolled into town with his entourage from Susa? As I thought about this, I realised that I come to this story with a lot of hindsight: I have the journal of Nehemiah to read; I have the cross of Jesus to refer to; I have the panoramic view of scripture. But these people were there, right in the middle of it, living it. They didn't know what a relationship with God looked like then. They had been living in broken rubble for 100 years. They had been living in a broken covenant for generations and generations, the very reason for their exile. Many of them were not familiar with the stories of their God or their people. Some of the locals didn't even speak Hebrew, they were so assimilated into the state of subjugation – both physically... but also spiritually, that their knowledge and understanding about their relationship was so very poor.

Instead of expecting the people to catch up to where Nehemiah was as he rides into town, immersed in prayer, and plans and purposes, Nehemiah was taking the people on a journey. He's taking them along this way, along this road map towards restoration.

There is a journey that they are making towards a stronger relationship with God. They needed to understand more about their relationship with God. They needed to see how God is working to restore and rebuild their homes. They needed to bear witness to more and more of what the vision of this covenant is. He is keeping in mind that the vision Nehemiah is rebuilding was always about the relationship; that's the goal.

Spoken and Action

We see that there are two dimensions to this covenant being put in place. The passage describes the *spoken declaration*, their verbal commitment to this relationship covenant. The heads of the tribes and families are listed as they place their seal to this covenant.

It also describes *Action* – what they *do* to demonstrate their commitment to his relationship covenant: "We will not neglect the house of our God". Life was not going to go back to their old normal. There is a new normal that is now part of their lives.

Tithes and offerings were being received. First fruit offerings were being received. Musicians supported a lifestyle of worship. This is not just *spoken* – talking about it, this is also *action*, that carried into every aspect of their lives. Life and lifestyle had turned a corner.

Am I more focused on spoken – what I say, or Action – what I do?

Underpinning love

Always, there is this under-pinning, under-current, under-girding of love. Healthy Relationship in action – with God and with each other. Care and compassion, loving God, loving others. This was the vision that Nehemiah was rebuilding. This is the vision that God had for the old Jerusalem, a place of *salem*, a place of *peace*. It is the vision that God has for the new Jerusalem, a place of *salem*, a place of peace, when Jesus returns.

Some final thoughts...

In the process of rebuilding spiritual strength, strengthening our relationship with God, Nehemiah identified that there were some significant and powerful steps that required that to progress.
> **Confession** – saying sorry and having other bear witness to that.
> **Covenant** – renewing their commitment to the love relationship also before witnesses.

These are the things that were stones for building spiritual strength in this community of people.

At one church where we worked, we were having continual difficulties with the guttering. After rain, the guttering would weaken and fall off the fascia where it was attached. We'd put it back up again, which worked until the next tropical downpour. After investigation, we found that there was blockage in the drainage and the weight of the water in the guttering during a storm was too much for the screws to hold it. This became a major project of digging up the drainage to the street to find the source of the problem. When the downpipe was removed a foot-long plug of silt and sludge gushed out, along with a tennis ball or two. The smell of that muck was awful! It had been clogged for probably decades. After it was cleared, fresh rainfall could run out unhindered to the street because the blockage had been cleared.

Confession and repentance are like getting rid of the plug of silt and sludge that prevents the fresh flow of the Spirit in our lives. It can be a build-up of little things, or it can be from some big balls of sin that cause the blockage. It is an uncomfortable, messy process, but necessary if we are going to have the flow of clear water to those around us.

Nehemiah was not just working in a civic space – rebuilding a place where people could live. Not was it just an administrative space – governing fair processes. Nor was it just a cultural space, where they could express and celebrate their Hebrew traditions. Nehemiah's work was also a spiritual one. He took the steps that were needed to restore and strengthen their spiritual relationship with God. He didn't balk at implementing what he knew would clear the conduit so that the clear, fresh water of life could flow through their city once more.

Prayer:

Father God, we thank you that you are compassionate, loving and merciful. You bear witness to our journey, even in all of our limitations and weaknesses. We know that you desire us to be people where the water of life and run freely to those around us. Forgive us for the things that have caused blockages in our relationship with you. As I pray this, I think of .... and I am so sorry. Forgive me for .... and help me to make right what is in my power to correct. Thank you for your everlasting love; help me to walk in greater freedom, unhindered by the mistakes of the past because of your grace and forgiveness.

In Jesus Name, Amen.

9.

Town was reoccupied

Where we are up to...

Our journey with Nehemiah as he had a vision to rebuild Jerusalem and to lift its people out of shame, is coming to an end. We have seen remarkable changes from that very first review he had of the city as he rode his horse around the city seeing broken rubble and exposed sections of the wall. There are now a strong administration and processes to protect the city and its people. The cultural fabric of their community was starting to feel like home again. They have reconnected with their relationship with God and have recommitted to the covenant with Him.

But Nehemiah notices another problem. And that problem was that everything was in place except one important thing: People. The streets were empty.

All these other actions were there for the place to function for the people. So, Nehemiah oversees a strategic and intentional plan to address this. He sets about ensuring that the town is reoccupied.

Bible Reading
Nehemiah 11:1-4

The town was re-occupied with Workers

Nehemiah provides us with a summary of the census of the people who relocated to live in Jerusalem. If we add up the numbers documented, it comes to 3044 adult men. These are workers – people with positions and occupations with responsibilities to fulfil.

Most of the men noted in this account are leaders of the people, some have a direct line to Emperor Artaxerxes, like Nehemiah who is Governor. But there are also others that automatically came with them. With each of these people there were accompanying households, women and children, domestics and attendants.

The 10% strategy

The number 10% is a familiar for us. Immediately this reminds us of the tithe, which is 10% of our income given to God and his work. 10% of the people move from outlying communities into Jerusalem. Some of these were identified by casting lots. Some of them volunteered to move and relocate.

What I notice is that Nehemiah did not wait for this reoccupation of the city to happen by a natural process of drift. This was intentional, considered and strategic. This process did not just swell Jerusalem by 3000, but some commentators rise that number up into the vicinity of 20,000.

What we have now is not just a rebuilt walled city. This is an occupied community – thriving, moving, working, functioning, operating, performing. Fulfilling what it was designed to accomplish. Fulfilling the original vision.

The town was re-occupied with Worshipers

And then tucked away in Chapter 11 there is a rather unusual comment:

Bible Reference
Nehemiah 11:23

This is a massive shift from the same king who had shut down the rebuilding of the city wall that we read about previously in Ezra. A lifestyle and culture of worship of God is now not just tolerated, it is promoted.

What place does worship have in my journey of rebuilding?

The opposition and reports of treason against Nehemiah have lost their influence. In Ezra there is a record of correspondence from King Artaxerxes who exempted the priests, temple servants and musicians from Persian taxes.

What is it like to recognise that God can turned opposition into positioning and influence?

Bible Reference
Ezra 7:24

This is evidence of more movement. This was a huge dispensation of grace. Jerusalem is no longer just tolerated, it is embraced. Not just embraced, but those who worked in the temple were given leave from the burden of taxes. Not just exempt from taxes but provided for out of the royal treasury. The king was pulling resources from the Empire and pouring it into Jerusalem's culture of worship.

Is there a stronger affirmation that this city, with its lifestyle of worship, is a point of strength for this community? What had been opposition how now moved and transformed into positioning and influence.

Place of Worth

Now Jerusalem is recognised as a point of strength – not just a healthy city but it is recognised as good for the Empire. It is a jewel in the Persian Empire and a place of worth. It enhances the whole Empire. Why else would King Artaxerxes advocate for it so?

The shame and distress that Nehemiah heard about years ago in Susa, has finally been lifted. No longer are people covering their eyes when they mention Jerusalem. But now there is a tone of pride and of satisfaction. Where they may have said, *"Oh... ahh, yes... there's Jerusalem..."* Now it is: *"Jerusalem is part of our Empire! It is a thriving, healthy, wonderful place. That is part of what we do here!"*

Some final thoughts...

Nehemiah went through all these steps because God gave him a vision to rebuild. That vision was not just for a great location and a good venue. The city was strong and secure, beautiful and pleasing, but most of all, it was a vision for the people. He saw that this vision needed people and he went about intentionally reoccupying the town.

I notice that reoccupation happened towards the end of this account. Sometimes I think we can be so anxious for people, that we can be tempted to push the people-agenda without the structures to support them. But people need a place with all of these structures, so that they feel safe, and feel that they belong, and they feel that they matter, that this is their place.

Jerusalem was now filled with people. This was now a city worth owning and acknowledging and supporting and belonging to. That is a big ship to turn around. But Nehemiah caught what God saw, and believed it was possible, and immersed himself into this "good work" (he called it that) with all of his heart.

Prayer:

Father God that you intend us to live in community, thriving with healthy relationships in multiple layers. Help me to know what my part is in being part of a healthy family, a healthy church and faith community, and a healthy neighbourhood, town and nation. We pray your blessing over all of these circles we are part of and ask that you would continue to bless these as thriving, healthy communities.
In Jesus Name, Amen.

10.
Ceremony and Celebration

Where we are up to...

Now people are living and working and thriving in Jerusalem! They had achieved so much to get to this point. This is something worth celebrating, so let's look at how they did that.

Bible Reading
Nehemiah 12:27-43

Celebrate milestones

This community did not arrive at this point in 52 days. They didn't stay in a mindset of picking up the pieces. They didn't stay in a state of mourning and confession. They went through all of these milestones, following the map they were given by Nehemiah who saw the value and necessity of these places and they attended to those matters well. But now their due diligence has paid off.

Now there is a time to pause and to look back and say, *"Wow! Look where God has brought us from!"* Now there is a time to pause and to look around and declare *"Wow! Look what God has accomplished through us here!"* Now there is a time to pause and to look forward and anticipate *"Wow! Look where God is taking us!"*

I have had many conversations where I encourage people to acknowledge and celebrate their wins. I've noticed that Australians, on the whole, are pretty reluctant to celebrate wins, to celebrate successes, to celebrate what has gone well. Perhaps it is an Australian thing that we don't go around big-noting success because we fear it comes across as arrogant.

Perhaps there is also an element of fear: Don't dwell on the good, because it probably won't last. Or even superstition: name it and you'll jinx it. But this celebration is a Godly thing to do! This was an acceptable, completely appropriate God honouring act! Nehemiah understood very clearly that to celebrate this milestone of success was right. Absolutely right!

What success or achievement of milestones do I need celebrate?

Ceremony

The way they do this is to dedicate the rebuilt walls and gates to the purposes of God. They do this with the most extravagant display of pomp and ceremony. It is solemn; it is serious; it is significant; but it also looks like a carnival, a festival, a party, fireworks. This is an extravaganza!

There is music, and choirs, and orchestras, costumes and dignitaries. This was not a half-cooked, slapped-together, crack open a bottle or two, kind of event. This was an occasion! It was honouring, organised, excellence, brilliant, distinguished. The sound of this party in Jerusalem could be heard far away! This was a big bash!

Symbolic track of the Choir

I love the picture of the two choirs walking around the top of the walls, walking the circumference of the city and meeting together at the House of God. This ceremony is also a symbolic walk – from the southern part of the wall, down where the dung gate was, walking along the parameter of the wall in two groups up to the north aspect of the sheep gate, through the gate into the temple courts.

They have been on a journey of restoration, from the depths of pain and distress, towards wholeness and community and health. This ceremonial parade of musicians has been used as an analogy that also maps our own course in our journey towards God. We start down near the dung gate, far away from God, in our own filth, as it were and we move towards God entering in through the Sheep Gate.

How would I describe my own journey of salvation from the dung gate to the courts of joy through the Sheep Gate?

The Sheep Gate was the way that the sacrificial lambs were taken into the temple to offer redemption, so that the people could also enter into the courts of worship with singing and joy and celebration with God.

Bible Reading
John 10:7

Jesus said, "I am the gate for the sheep. I am *the* gate; to be saved, you have to enter into God's presence through me..."

This is a bold statement where Jesus declares he is the Christ with great emphasis. He is 'The Gate'. Not just any gate, but this gate! The way of salvation and redemption. The way of reconciliation with God the Father. The way into God's presence. Every Jew knew that they had entry into the presence of God within the Temple because of the blood of the sacrificial lambs that entered through that Sheep Gate. Jesus declares that He is that portal into God's presence.

This celebration of the restoration work in Jerusalem prophetically recognises this spiritual truth. We can try all sorts of routes to move away from the Dung Gate. However, if we are to get into that place of peace and reconciliation and joy, there is only one effective route: we need to go through the Sheep Gate. Through Jesus. There is no other way.

What sort of things have I tried to move my life away from the Dung Gate?

Some final thoughts...

So much has been happening in Jerusalem during Nehemiah's time as governor, and it culminates in this powerful and magnificent celebration. The people come together and really rejoice! It was dedication that the wall had been successfully restored. It was a marker of celebrating their success as a people coming back to occupy the promises of God. Nehemiah is rebuilding a vision of a people who were occupying Jerusalem, strong and secure. What a wonderful opportunity to celebrate being the people of God!

Prayer:

Thank you, Father God that you are the source of all good things in our life, particularly our salvation through Jesus who is the Gate. Thank you that in acknowledging the milestones of good in our life, we are also acknowledging your generous goodness which you have given us. Help us to hold that fine line of honouring you and not slip into arrogance. We honour you and we love you,
In Jesus Name, Amen.

11.

Ongoing Process of Checking the Vision

Where we are up to...

Our journey with Nehemiah has come to an end. God gave him a vision to rebuild Jerusalem and to lift its people out of shame, and we have witnessed remarkable changes during the twelve years he was governor.

They overcame incredible opposition to see the wall repaired. The city is now thriving. It is an administration centre. There are people living there, working there, worshiping there. We have seen the ten stages of rebuilding that Nehemiah went through. This would seem to be quite an appropriate place to close the book, with the wonderful celebration that happened at the dedication of the rebuilt wall, and we all go home.

However, what we find is that this account does not end at Chapter Twelve with the celebration. There is, almost symbolically, a Chapter Thirteen. Nehemiah's account is not the white-washed social media version of the story. There is realism in this account, with the high-lights and the low-lights. The parts of victory and the difficult parts.

So, before we finish, we will have a look at this final chapter as we wrap up our reflections of Nehemiah.

Bible Reference
Nehemiah 7:2

Nehemiah has appointed a successor, a godly man of integrity. There is a functioning succession plan, the points to note is that Nehemiah was looking for men of integrity and the fear of God. They were the first qualities that he was after. He has appointed his brother Hanani, not because of nepotism, but because Hanani has been on this journey with him. It was his brother's report that activated this whole process. Nehemiah also appointed the commander of the citadel or palace, a God-fearing man with administrative expertise and experience.

After the wonderful highpoint of celebration, Nehemiah returns to Susa according to his commitment to King Artaxerxes, to work for him. There is no doubt, that even though his time as Governor in Jerusalem was a civic appointment according to the view of the government at the time – that this was first and foremost, a God appointment for a period of specialised, specific ministry. So, when that mission was completed, he returned again to civilian life in Susa – working in the court of the emperor, as he had arranged with him, right at the beginning.

Bible Reading
Nehemiah 13:1-12

Reforms at the Temple

But then Nehemiah hears of some distressing deviations had started to become practiced again, and he returns to Jerusalem. And it is here that we find things have gradually, incrementally gone off course. Although there were processes in place, it seems there was required an additional emphasis required to keep checking-in. The final aspect of rebuilding was to have regular check-ins to see how they were standing with the original vision.

Stephen R. Covey [iii] suggests that when we take an aeroplane trip to any particular predetermined destination, when we are in the air the plane is, in fact, off course at least 90% of the time. All sort of conditions, such as weather and turbulence cause it to get off track. However, the aeronautical instruments constantly give feedback to the pilot, who then makes corrections and adjustments. They keep coming back to the precise flight plan, bringing the plane back on course. Often, the plane arrives at the destination on time, because of this vigilance in keep coming back to the original vision or intention.

The flying "1 in 60 rule," states that for every 1 degree off course error, the plane will miss its target by 1 mile for every 60 miles flown. That means that without this constant correction, even a very small deviation, such as only 1° off course, will have you over 250 miles away from where you intended to be, by the time you circumnavigate the globe.

Getting off track is not really the problem, that's part of our life 'flight' experience, as long as we are vigilant in readjusting our course back to the original template and vision that God provides us with.

Can I identify where I am off course, even just a small amount?

This chapter starts with the reading of scripture. If the people know the stories, they understand the principles. If they understand the principles, they can apply the truth. If they apply the truth, then what they do, will reflect that.

Transformational

This is a transformational process, not a transactional one. Transformation is a process that happens at a DNA level. I am changed; love and truth and grace become part of the way I do life.

Nehemiah was a transformational Governor. He looked for people who feared God. He did not take the role because of what he could get out of it, or what it would do for him, but because he was positioned to see a vision translated into the hearts of the people. What he discovers as he returns to Jerusalem, is that the transformation and commitment to the vision had stalled. Stopped. The diligence to keep checking in has not been completed.

There were probably pockets where things that had been rebuilt were still enduring. Obviously, the walls hadn't fallen over, but there were some serious deviations from God's vision. And this is what he returns to address.

Transactional

A Transactional style of living – in relationships and in religion, is a process of performing to achieve your outcomes. I pay my way: I do this for you, and in return, you will do stuff for me. It is doing something with a price attached. It is scratching my back and I will scratch yours.

This is the way that Tobiah did life. Remember that we have met Tobiah before: he was an Ammonite, and now he is living and residing in the House of God. He transacted his way into making the Temple of God his personal opulent residence. He moved in and moved the offering and tithe stores out. He influenced for his own gain. He was tight with the high priest and used that relationship for his own influence.

Am I more prone to trying to transact change in my life, by bargaining and using leverage?

Everything about this is wrong! Yet those who were there allowed it to continue. They refused to see this as 'sin'.

Staying on Track

So how do we stay on track? How do we stay true to the course God has set for us, and not get lured off into a degree of falsehood that eventually lands us nowhere near where we intended to be?

We mentioned that this chapter starts with the reading of scripture. They were reading a story that occurred during the Exodus, which is recorded in Numbers.

Bible Reference
Numbers 22-24; 25:1-3

Balaam was a witch doctor and heathen priest who had been hired by the King of Moab to curse the people of I as they were crossing the plains of Moab during the Exodus. However, God turned the curses of Balaam into a blessing. Balaam literally could not speak out curses over God's people.

So, the people of Moab chose another strategy, a back door strategy to break down the moral and physical strength of the Israelites. They had the Moabite women seduce the Israelite men to engage in sexual religious orgies, and to defile themselves by worshiping at the altars of foreign gods. This act opened them up to vulnerability, spiritually and physically. The cost of this act of unfaithfulness was high. Many people died. Moses then wrote a law against intermarrying. This was a law that was not just about racial intolerance, it was putting a boundary around their personal purity and fidelity to God.

After Nehemiah had this story read to his people, they understood. They understood what it meant to be faithful to God. All in, not just a bit of this here and there, not just as it suits. The Israelites separated themselves again, devoted solely to God. The way they expressed that was separating themselves apart from the other cultures and versions of religion around them.

Nehemiah again establishes sweeping reforms, putting God first. How do we do stay in that place? How do we stay close to the original vision? What keeps us aligned to what God has designated as the best way to do life? One way is to remind ourselves of the stories in the Bible. What does the Word of God lay out? What happened? How did that look back then? What was God's response? If we understand God's word, we will understand His heart. And if we understand His heart, we will be motivated to do what we can to protect this relationship with Him.

Some people read this account and only see a judgemental God, intolerant of other cultures, a God of exclusion. But we are told God is a God of love. His heart is for all people. He is setting this up, so all people will understand his heart. In his wisdom there is a process, there is a timeline moving towards the cross of Jesus to a New Covenant that will open up this relationship to all people.

However, to these people, in this era, embracing other cultures in Jerusalem looked like changing a place of holy worship to be someone's personal residence so he could make a statement about his influence and power. What the priest Eliashib allowed was not okay. Nehemiah is not understating it when he says what Eliashib allowed was "evil". The temple of God was never meant to be a personal home of indulgence. The temple was a template of God's sacred grace and movement towards people.

This side of the Cross and Pentecost we understand that God's Holy Spirt indwells people of any race. People can worship in living-rooms and offices and backyards. But right here, in this time, they are not there yet.

Nehemiah's returns to the original vision. He goes back to the things he had already put in place and again regulates the reforms. He evicts Tobiah – he throws his stuff out on the street in a dramatic statement.

He has the priests ceremonially cleanse the rooms. He reclaims the space so it could be used for what it was intended for – a place to hold the offerings and the tithes for the house of God because there had been nowhere for these offerings to be stored, giving had dried up.

Nehemiah reviews the payments from the emperor's treasury – we read about these previously. They were intended to pay the Levites and musicians. He finds these payments had not been made where they were budgeted. There was also the allocation of tithes and offerings under Mosaic law for their support that were not being given to them. If the Levites were not getting their allowance, they could not support their families. This put them in a position where their households would go hungry. They would be destitute. Most had gone back to work in their fields to support themselves. In this agrarian era, they could not do both. There was no such thing as a bi-vocational Levite.

Nehemiah fixes the Tobiah problem, and the offerings start to pour in again. I notice that the people were willing to give, but there had been nowhere for them to put these offerings, so that they gave up turning up, just to be turned away.

Bible Reading
Nehemiah 13: 15-22

Reforms regarding the Sabbath

God's law works with us and for us, not against us to make our lives problematic.

I wonder if there is such a high incidence of burn-out and mental health issues because of the pace of our world. Life without rest – physical rest, or mental rest has become the expected. It is easy to take no Sabbath in our week. Hectic, busy, flat-out, frantic, exhausted, full-on, hard, these are common ways people describe their normal.

STOP: Sabbath Rest

God has instilled in us a need to draw aside, not just for an annual holiday, but on a regular basis, on the basis of this week. Those rhythms of work and rest had been discarded again. God designed our physical, mental and spiritual bodies to have a down time, a day off to rest, a day off to commune. If we don't, we leave ourselves vulnerable again.

Press PAUSE

These merchants in Nehemiah's day were in the same boat. They believed they had to kept going. They didn't know how to press pause. They were no longer slaves in the physical sense, but they were driven by the pursuit of more. Productivity had become their slavedriver. This was another form of slavery.

People told me during the Covid-19 pandemic when everything was shut down, that they didn't know how to do that. They didn't know how to be still, quiet. Their lives had come to a screeching halt, and it was disturbing. They had not experienced the idea of pressing pause before and it forced them to think about what they wanted to keep and what they wanted to resume when it was over.

Personally, I didn't find it too disruptive. Necessity had already taught me to pause. Certainly, it was inconvenient, but the level of personal disturbance was not high for me because it was already part of the rhythm I was used to. I'm not saying that a global pandemic was a good thing; it hurt many, many people but the idea of pressing pause, on a regular basis, on a weekly basis, becoming familiar with that and how to do that is not just a good idea, that is a God idea. God put that in place long before shutdowns were imposed. His intention was that it would become a life-habit for our own wellbeing.

Where do I need to press PAUSE?

These merchants were the same. They felt it was too hard to stop. They felt they couldn't afford Sabbath; that it had to do more; they had to work; they had to earn more; they had deadlines to meet; they had targets to reach. They objected to Nehemiah's enforcement of the sabbath and camped outside the city gates in protest.

Yet, we see how Nehemiah did make it possible. He pressed pause for them. Sun-down to Sun-down, until the Sabbath was over. He had the gatekeepers close the gates to the city. He threatened to arrest them for loitering if they hung around. Huh. That will do it. They managed to work in that pause after-all.

GO: Check the windows and doors.

There was no point having a wall rebuilt and intact, with all the gates strong and solid and intact, when they were opened willy-nilly to let anything in at any time of day, for any purpose. These gates had been dedicated to the purposes of God, but the people had let those purposes slide.

The one of the first good purposes to go, was to worship and honour of God. They had not stopped to check if what they were doing was in line with God's best. Checking in like this is a process that I call "checking the windows and doors". They didn't review or challenge or evaluate the status of things.

Do I have a process in my life to check how I am tracking with God?

Yet, as soon as Nehemiah is back in Jerusalem, he identifies what things need to be re-evaluated. He addresses them positively, definitely, purposefully.

Reforms in Life

There were also some other points in which reforms were implemented, which we have touched on before.

Bible Reading
Nehemiah 13:23-28

Language

One of the big indicators that Nehemiah could see things were swaying away from the original vision was the language that was spoken. It was the same as the nations around them. These people no longer could speak kingdom, the language of Judah. They spoke heathen dialects, their children only learn to speak like those around them.

If the people are primarily speaking the dialect of the nations around them, then there is a good indicator, that they are not immersing themselves in matters of their own kingdom.

Is my language like the people around me, or am I careful about the words that I choose?

Are my words kind, positive, thoughtful, encouraging?

Unequally yoked

There was another boundary that God had given the people: marry like-minded people; kingdom with kingdom. In the New Testament we would call that not being 'unequally yoked'.

Bible Reference
2 Corinthians 6:14

I remember responding to a Christian blog post that proposed that interfaith marriages were a legitimate expression of unity and an expression of God's family in action. His idea was not just between variations of Christian faith expressions such as Catholics with Baptists, but Christians with non-Christians, such as Hindus, Muslims and so on. I don't usually get involved in these types of opinion pieces, but this disturbed me. I responded, very politely, because I didn't understand how he interpreted scripture this way. "If this was okay, why was Nehemiah so upset about intermarriages?"
The response was, "I'm not a theologian but I'm guessing you are referring to the passage in the New Testament about being unequally yoked..." and he proceeded to defend (respectfully) his position. He had missed my thought completely. My contention is this: I don't have a doctorate in theology either, but I am familiar with the stories of the Bible. And Nehemiah's story was waving a very red flag in the face of this position. Not because we don't love other people, regardless of their faith stance, but because there is a principle of faithfulness to God that can be jeopardised, and it is best to avoid it, if we have control over this decision. This can steer us off by degrees and we will not land where we intend to go.

I believe this unequally yoking is not just a boundary around marriage, but any significant partnership, such as business, or close friendships. Nehemiah states that if there was ever a person who could be considered above this directive it would have been King Solomon, wise, educated, astute, rich and famous. But his undoing, in Kingdom of God terms, was being unequally yoked. Marrying and getting into bed with those who did not honour or follow God does not work. It drew Solomon away from the original vision, God's flight plan. It will do the same for you.

No one is exempt from God's law, not even the King Solomons of this world, the rich, the powerful, the clever, the educated. Nehemiah, using the story of Solomon as a caution, acknowledges the same thing was happening again.

Am I yoked to people who do not honour God? How do I hold myself on course in these relationships?

Loyalty to God

Loyalty was a reoccurring issue. Over and over, as this comes up in scripture, the issue was not the marriages *per se*... but the way in which these relationships diluted the truth in their lives. This was not a form of fascist racial purity; this was the portal to discarding God. Discarding God's values. Discarding his underpinning virtues. Truth becomes distorted. Loyalty to God becomes blurred. It happened to Solomon.

Even the wisest man on earth could not discern the truth when his household was immersed in ungodly cultures and religions.

Ezra had spent a great deal of time and energy addressing this same issue.

Bible Reference
Ezra 9:2

Ezra was so appalled by what was happening that he went into mourning. Rending his garments, pulling out his hair and his beard. Nehemiah was so grieved that he went into a rage, only not using those cultural expressions against himself, he does that to those who were unrepentant in this matter. Nehemiah was truly disgusted, just like Ezra before him.

Was his response culturally appropriate? I'm guessing it was it was so potent and intense that it got their attention. They understood that he was extremely serious about this. Would this be an appropriate response now, to express our zeal for God in such a way? No, I don't think so. Plucking beards is not an approach for pastoral care we should consider. What it does suggest though, is to challenge how serious we are about not diluting our loyalty to God.

How do I stay near to the heart of God, being loyal and true?

Some final thoughts...

Here we conclude our journey with Nehemiah. God gave him a vision to rebuild a wall, and a city but most of all, a vision for the people. When the vision was fulfilled, it was such a magnificent milestone to celebrate. But without ongoing vigilance and checking the windows and doors, the people very quickly got off track. They deviated from the original flight plan and landed a long way from where they intended to be. Learning and knowing the stories in Scripture helped them to identify what was important and to address those things.

Nehemiah is rebuilding a vision of a people who were occupying Jerusalem with passion and loyalty to God. What a wonderful opportunity recognised that God has included us to be part of his vision to rebuild the Kingdom of God where he has positioned us.

Prayer:

Father God, thank you for the account of Nehemiah, and all of the things we have been able to draw out of this story. Thank you that your truth is so palatable when we understand your intention is always love towards us. Thank you that your truth leads us toward freedom, not slavery. As we reflect further on this story, bring to our awareness where we need to align ourselves according to your flight plan, so that we will arrive at the destination where you want us to be.
In Jesus Name, Amen.

Appendix A
The Stages of Nehemiah's Rebuilding Framework

	STAGE	REFERENCE
1	THE VISION WAS CAUGHT	NEHEMIAH 1
2	THE MISSION WAS ACCEPTED	NEHEMIAH 1
3	GAPS AND NEEDS WERE ASSESSED	NEHEMIAH 2
4	OPPOSITION WAS OVERCOME	NEHEMIAH 4
5	THE WALL STRUCTURE WAS REBUILT	NEHEMIAH 3, 6
6	PROCESSES WERE REINSTATED	NEHEMIAH 5, 7
7	CULTURE WAS RE-ESTABLISHED	NEHEMIAH 8
8	SPIRITUAL STRENGTH WAS DEVELOPED (CONFESSION AND COMMITMENT)	NEHEMIAH 9, 10
9	THE TOWN WAS REOCCUPIED	NEHEMIAH 11
10	THE WALLS AND GATES WERE DEDICATED (CEREMONY AND CELEBRATION)	NEHEMIAH 12
11	ONGOING PROCESS OF CHECKING THE VISION	NEHEMIAH 13

Other books in this Series

Endnotes

[i] www.myjewishlearning.com
Article: What Is Shmita, the Sabbatical Year?
https://www.myjewishlearning.com/article/what-is-shemita-the-sabbatical-year/

[ii] Matthew 6:33

[iii] Stephen R. Covey, How to Develop Your Personal Mission Statement

www.ingramcontent.com/pod-product-compliance
Lightning Source LLC
Chambersburg PA
CBHW040108100526
44584CB00029BA/3952